818
M   Morgan, Henry

        DOGS

HENRY MORGAN

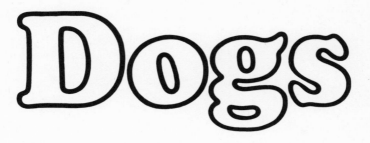

GEORGE BOOTH

HOUGHTON MIFFLIN COMPANY BOSTON

1977

Library of Congress Cataloging in Publication Data
Morgan, Henry, 1915-   Dogs.
1. Dogs — Anecdotes, facetiae, satire, etc.
I. Booth, George, 1926-   II. Title.
PN6231.D68M57   818'.5'407   75-41449
ISBN 0-395-24207-X   ISBN 0-395-25169-9 (pbk.)
Printed in the United States of America

C 10 9 8 7 6 5

Booth's funnies is dedicated

to Uncle Ray

Henry says, "me too"

A History (ON THE DULL SIDE)

Your ancient Egyptians thought of the dog as hot stuff. They were the folks who named Syrius the "dog-star" because when Sirius showed up it meant that the Nile was going to overflow again . . . something that it did quite faithfully in the days before the Aswan Dam.

It was this regularity, or faithfulness, that led the simple farmers to think that the star was as dependable as a dog. This appears to be a bit on the odd side when one considers that Sirius shows up without anyone's having to whistle for it or feed it dinner.

All the other stars showed up regularly too, but this didn't seem to impress anybody. If a star appeared and the Nile didn't overflow, the hell with it.

The ancient Israelites didn't think much of the bow-wow. They believed it was wrong to worship idols and they didn't care for Pharaoh anyway. While the Hebrew chillun were out in the yard making bricks under the hot sun, Pharaoh's dog was inside sitting under the fan on a silk cushion eating date sherbet. Feelings ran high.

7

The Mohammedans and Hindus didn't like dogs either. Nor do they now. To them a dog is no better than a Christian, and a Christian is, simply, a "dog."

The Chinese, over the centuries, have had the habit of eating dogs. Mostly they wouldn't touch a Christian even if he were *en croûte* and served with a mousseline sauce.

The early Greeks had dogs and there is, according to the 1911 Encyclopaedia Britannica, a "beautiful piece of sculpture in the possession of Lord Feversham at Duncombe Hall, representing the favorite dog of Alcibiades. It looks like a Newfoundland."

This could mean that the Greeks discovered North America. Or that the Iroquois discovered Athens. Someone should look into it.

In old time Ethiopia the folks thought so much of dogs that they had an Abyssinian terrier as king. It could do anything a king could do merely by fawning or growling. In this way the dog (king) showed that he either liked what was going on or he didn't. Kings don't change.

It is not known if the throne could be inherited.

Today, according to the supermarket figures, the dog is still king. More canned dog food is sold each day than any other packaged product. And by a considerable margin. While somebody's child is eating a soybean burger and a fizzy drink, the dog is getting a full measure of vitamins, proteins and carbohydrates. People's children are getting weaker, as time goes on, and their dogs are getting stronger.

We see this as a hopeful sign and therefore have dedicated this book to the race of the future.

Then, perhaps, someday, man will find his rightful place in the sun:

"A dog's best friend."

Traits

Human people have a bad habit of lumping other people into groups and then making nasty remarks. French people are considered to be "different" from English people, and so on.

Dogs have better sense. A German shepherd doesn't think that a Welsh corgi is a crook. A Chihuahua doesn't hold Great Danes in contempt.

Oh, they'll fight, of course. But even then they don't try to wipe out whole breeds of dogs. Dobermans don't get together and decide that all dachshunds must go. Only individual dogs fight, and darn seldom at that. Perhaps the most common disputes between them are about things they've been taught by Man. "This is my yard. You keep out of it." The man, actually believing that he is the owner of a piece of earth, teaches this kind of nonsense to his

dog. No dog ever believed for a minute that he owned a meadow. Or a bush or a tree.

It's also a fact that dogs don't draw distinctions among other species of animal. You've been taught that dogs hate cats. Well, they don't. They like, some of them, to *chase* cats, and they like to *chase* rabbits and chipmunks and butterflies and, sometimes, even scraps of paper blowing in the wind. But this is not combativeness or even aggressiveness. Thousands of households have canaries and goldfish and gerbils and dogs and crickets and babies. They live together and they play together. Happily.

It may come as a surprise to some but there are no "vicious" dogs either. Not by nature, at any rate. The only time a dog is what we call vicious is when he is ill. Or, when he's been trained to be.

Dogs do not get to look like their owners. What happens is that people buy dogs who look like them.

Dogs have been known to eat pancakes, spaghetti, charcoal, ice, peppermints, grass, whatever. As a rule of thumb, if the dog eats it it won't hurt him. He knows more than you think he does.

The easiest way to train a dog is to start with yourself. If you can get yourself trained, the rest is pie.

While dogs don't get to look like their masters, they grow to be like them in some ways. Some times. If, for example, you are morose, after a bit Fido will be sort of droopy. A jolly fella usually has a jolly dog.

Are some breeds "smarter" than others? Authorities say not. But somehow, somewhere in the genes, there seem to be characteristics that differentiate one kind from another. After centuries of training, some of these dogs seem to be better at herding sheep than others. Maybe the others just don't care about sheep. Why, you take a collie who's never even seen a sheep, show him one, and just *see* if he cares. He won't herd it worth a tinker's tink.

Do dogs actually like people? Sure, but not in the same way that people like people. For a few thousand years dogs have been associated with people, but the odds are very good that the choice was made by the dogs. Nobody knows what the original Towser had in mind . . . whether it was the fairly steady menu, the roof over his head in rainy weather or merely that he found man a lot of laughs. We'll never know.

BOOTH

The Dachshund

This is the dachs or badger hound, especially designed to catch badgers for people who think they want one. Badger bristles make nice shaving brushes but nobody wants one any more. This leaves the dachs with a great deal of free time which he spends in making friends.

It is a fact that dachshunds aren't angry with anybody. Ever. They are especially not angry with Skye terriers, for example, and this often leads to a new dachs with long hair.

When the frankfurter was invented (in Frankfurt, more or less), the native folks, Frankfurters themselves, took one look and thought of our old buddy, mister low-slung. "Ach," they said, those of them who said things like that, "Ach. Ein heisser hund." The wienie *did* look like the dog, and it *was* hot. Hot dog.

Strangely enough the hot dog is also known as the "wiener." This is owing to the fact that Alt Wien was the pet name for Vienna and the hot dog was adopted by the people who also gave to the world the Wiener schnitzel.

Hamburgers are named for the city of Hamburg. This makes the cheeseburger impossible.

The Big Mac is named after Old McDonald.

(Isn't it fun that when you say "wienie" you're actually saying "little Vienna?")

BOOTH

The Collie

A breed that originated in Scotland. Today, of course, the leading exports of that country are known as Teacher's, Dewar's and so forth.

The collie comes in two main categories, rough coat and smooth (relatively) coat. The usual height is between 20 and 24 inches at the shoulder, and the usual weight is between 50 and 60 pounds.

Those collies who become movie and TV stars are shifty about their sex. Lassie, for example, is a boy.

When it comes right down to it, the collie isn't such a fine actor as many people seem to want to believe. Even Lassie is rather stiff of expression. She (he) can walk or run forward and even around corners, but that's about it, folks.

If we are to judge by this one actor alone and try to generalize the habits of all collies from this one in particular, we find that they aren't very gregarious. Lassie never brings anyone home to dinner, doesn't seem to have a peer group and doesn't even belong to the public library.

When the movies were in production there were actually three "Lassies" available at any one time with another always in training. The reason for having three is that a collie's attention span is limited and after shooting a scene two or three times, whichever one was playing the part seemed to lose interest. It would be necessary to give him a break — time to read, go to the bathroom or investigate a rosebush.

It isn't that all collies look the same, either. But it's easy to fool some of the people some of the time.

Besides, they used make-up on him.

Aspirin Dogs (MOON BAYERS)

Many people have theories about why a dog bays at the moon.

They are wrong.

There are many dogs that don't bay at anything, and that's just for openers. The saluki, for example. The saluki has a terribly fascinating history which could fill a page. Among the ancient Assyrians, historians tell us, he may or may not have been known at all, and that's only part of it.

No traces of the saluki have been found in the ruins of Ur, a very old city. Not much of Ur has been found, either. Some have wondered whether the Basenji is related to the saluki because of the similarity in name endings. Yes.

The real question seems to be, when did dogs begin? Another question, almost as good, is "where?"

In Egypt they felt very strongly about the cat. In Ethiopia, once, they had a dog made king. Or was it in Eritrea? One of those dumb places. The folly of making a dog king can easily be seen when it has been shown that a dog's attention span is about twenty minutes. If you come up to a dog-king with a petition and say there are twenty thousand names on it, you've lost your audience.

Here in the West many dogs are *named* King, or Prince, or Earl, but it isn't the same thing.

Very few dogs are named Ambassador, or even Alderman.

Nobody seems to know why.

BOOTH

The German Shepherd

Your typical German shepherd is a somewhat backward fellow who is set to minding flocks of Schäfe. Schäfe hang out in Wiesen and eat lots of nice grün Gras.

A German shepherd's idea of a good time is to lie on his back on some hillside at night and look at the Sterne.

He also enjoys the Mondschein.

These are a simple folk and live on a simple diet of Brot and Kaese and Wasser. Being outdoors all the time and eating nothing but plain food they often live to be twenty-nine or thirty.

One sometimes reads of a "wise old shepherd." Well, there aren't any. They just look old from being left out in the rain all the time. As for a shepherd's being "wise," that's not worth discussing.

In East Germany, the typical shepherd earns a ruble a day.

If he doesn't eat anything and doesn't buy any clothes, in fourteen years he can buy a Zis.

The Detective Dog

A very smart cookie. This was once a police dog but got promoted on merit.

The 'tec, as he is called, is useful in many ways. People are always saying things like "You can never find a policeman when you want one." This is what the 'tec is very good at. Once you have him trained, all you have to say to him is something like "Serpico! Cop! Find a cop!" (In Canada it's "Find a constable." Prices slightly higher.)

'Tecs are particularly noted for their work in the woods, where three-year-old children are constantly getting losted. Since three-year-olds are people who have noodles for parents, a good 'tec dog will go off and find the child, bark until help comes, then go back and bite the mother.

If the ground is covered with ice and snow your 'tec can be fitted out with little gumshoes. These are obtainable at Sprtling's (see Appendix).

(Oops. Appendix has been removed. Well then, try Macy's.)

Some 'tecs, first grade, have made lieutenant, but on the average they prefer to work in the field.

There was, of course, one hound who became an Inspector — but that's a dog of a different collar.

16

Hangdog

Hardly anybody ever actually goes so far as to hang a dog.

The Watch Dog

This is a distant cousin to the pointer. As a matter of fact, he *is* a pointer but he's no danger to partridges or pheasants.

This animal is especially bred for his work and needs no training. What he does is in his blood . . . and the finer the blood lines, the more accurate the dog.

Your typical hunter has only one watch and it's a pretty good one, so he doesn't like to wear it when he's out in the fields. Also, it's much harder to tell time by the sun than you think. Besides, there's not always a sun out to tell time *by*. This is where your watch dog comes in handy.

What you do is set twelve sticks upright in the ground in a large circle. Make one stick about six inches higher than the others. It stands for "twelve."

Now you place your dog in the exact center so that he faces the tallest stick. Let's say, for purposes of illustration, that the dog's name is "Gentlemen."

What you do now is get outside of the circle. Then you turn around and face the dog. Then you give the command: "Time, Gentlemen, time, please!"

The dog will then stick out his tail and turn, pointing to the current time. A really fine watch dog can point within one or two seconds of the exact time.

When summer comes, you merely set your dog one hour ahead, reversing the process in the fall.

Mr. G. Morfit of Baltimore, this country's leading authority, has a dog named "Split." He works in tenths of a second.

Mr. Morfit oils his dog once a month.

Schleppenwulf

A city dweller. One of the few dogs bred strictly for laughs.

Your typical schlepper likes to hang around places where large numbers of people are in constant motion, such as supermarkets. He likes to accompany ladies while they push their shopping carts around the parking lot. He has enormous curiosity concerning what they have in their bundles.

A true intellectual, as are many products of mixed marriages, he has no interest in children. Tots like to pester him and he likes to bite them. Since he has a large brain he never actually bites any kid but you can tell from his expression what he's thinking.

Although no true schleppenwulf will ever go so far as to get into your car, he likes odds and ends from whatever you've bought . . . a raisin, a half doughnut, the end of a Hershey bar, etc.

BOOTH

In truth, the schlep lives a sort of hand-to-mouth existence and he wouldn't have it any other way. From your hand to his mouth.

One thing not in his favor is that he hasn't any true sense of loyalty. With him the A&P is just as good as Stop & Shop, and he'll abandon both in a second if he hears that there's more action at Safeway.

At one time he would have been called an egghead.

BOOTH

Air Dale

The pilot's best friend.

Airlines don't seem to understand about the air dale and won't allow him in the cockpit. This is too bad because the dog has a wonderful sense of direction. He's a kind of four-legged homing pigeon and always knows where he's been. You can blindfold him and take him a thousand miles away; still, when he gets back home he knows where your slippers are.

The main thing about this breed is that they really *love* air. Very often you'll see one riding in a car. If there's an open window, his head will be out it. He loves breathing and no matter how fast you drive, he keeps egging you on. He likes to feel his ears flying. If you go fast enough his ears stick straight out and he thinks he's an aircraft and it makes him feel swell.

Even as far back as the First World War, about 1917 say, flyers knew about this type of animal and when airplanes circled one another to see how things were going it was called a "dogfight."

Now it's true that dogs fight sometimes, but it's a strange undertaking. They never fight over money, for example. No dog wants to own another country, or oilwells, or silks and spices. The average dog doesn't want to own anything at all.

They really shouldn't fight.

It's silly.

Where do you suppose they learned it?

Mein Chow

Many people think that this dog is Chinese, but the fact is that it was bred originally in San Francisco for the China *trade*.

The original chow, a big eater, *was* Chinese, or is. He is, or was, somehow related to the Siberian husky.

(Husky is not a real name. It is the white man's way of saying, in effect, "That's a real dog you got there, Nuknuk.")

The Mein Chow is also related to the Yut Gar Mein and the Char Su Ding. As a group they are called the dogs of Fo. (Fo is pronounced more like "Foo," but in English that gives a peculiar impression.)

One of the less interesting things about the China trade is that at one time the port of Acapulco was the Pacific terminus. Spanish galleons would go to the Philippines (they weren't allowed *near* China) and swap Mexican silver for Chinese export dishes and soup tureens. From Acapulco the stuff was taken overland by burros to Vera Cruz and then on to Spain. It sounds like a lot of trouble but the fact of the matter is that the silver didn't cost them anything, bloody wogs did all the labor and the court of Spain lived like a king.

Later, the British took over most of the business by swapping the Chinese opium for their goods. They (Brit.) took a lot of tea in exchange for the opium but nobody in England had ever even heard of tea. The British East India Company got around that problem by taking out big ads in the Manchester *Guardian*, i.e.: "Does thy vain and haughty Mistress turn a deaf ear to thine importunities? Offer her a cup of brisk, ingratiating tea, and see!"

The first dogs imported from the Chinese mainland were called "coolies" because they were made to work like dogs.

"Coolies" built the transcontinental railway at a weekly wage of one dollar. When the railway was finished, they were killed.

Pique

Peking is pronounced Bay-ping, but if you start to throw your weight around with this you find that your dinner partner becomes restive.

Once upon a time the pique was a lap dog (Q.V.) and sat on the knees of empresses. They could possibly do other things but nobody ever saw them do them. You can read the whole history of the Far East back to whatsisname and you'll never see a word about the pique's doing anything but sitting. It's confusing anyway because the characters for "pique" can be read as either "lap dog," "withering" or "steam-driven device."

Professor Widdershins complains that there was no such thing as a steam engine at that time. Well, if you go back over what's been said you'll see that there is no reference to any particular time, so what's he talking about?

Dogs always end up looking like their masters, or a lot of people think that they do. If you look at a pique you can tell right off that it used to sit with or on an empress. The dog has the same look of hauteur, the same slightly offended air, the same stare of disapproval.

It is also usually taking offense, showing displeasure, suffering irritation and feeling resentment. It has a high, shrill voice which it uses to annoy people, many of whom think of it as a mean, rotten little dog. It is.

Piques have long hair which is used principally for shedding.

The female is called "pique-dame."

After considering the matter both pro (none) and con (plenty), it appears that the little animal is really good for just one thing — sitting on the lap of an empress.

Trick Dogs

Tall, suave, glistening — these are the hallmarks of one of the finest breeds in the world. They are magicians.

First you start with the small stuff: pulling a hat out of a rabbit, for instance. As you go along, see what it is that the magician does naturally and then all you have to do is the final polishing.

In two or three weeks your dog can learn the other basics of the trade. Sawing a dog in half is a good one. It stands to reason that an animal that can be trained to "play dead" can just as easily, with only a bit more effort, be taught to play Hamlet.

One of the easiest and most mutually enjoyable "tricks" you can teach is how to rush into a supermarket, grab a couple of steaks and run out again under the turnstile. This is done only in the off hours, of course, because few things will break a dog's spirit as much as having to stand in line behind a fat lady who's just bought her normal, or hundred-and-fifty-dollar weekend list. It is best to teach him early on that the best way in and out is at the *ends* — where the chains are.

Naturally, it needn't *always* be meat. A dog can get bored too,

you know. Once you've built up his confidence in the meat department, you can begin letting him vary the routine . . . ice cream, perhaps, or a gallon of milk. Some dogs appreciate it if they're allowed to go into their own special section of the store and grab a bucket of Toasty Nibbles, or whatever.

A Mrs. Blanny of New York City has "Melba," a wonderful companion who is very successful at rolling drunks.

Right from
the Beagle's Mouth

(World-famous Snoopy R. Beagle was kind enough to answer a few questions and his words bark for themselves. If anything is amiss, we apologize to his dear friend, Mr. Schulz.)

DEAR SIR:
Must get this off in a rush as it is raining. Briefly, my writing skill probably was inherited from my great-great uncle, or more, William Makepeace Beagle. On my mother's side, by the way, we are pretty much direct descendants of the winner of the Great War of 1066, William the Beagle.

As far as flying is concerned, we have quite a distinguished background. Beagle von Zeppelin was the builder of the first successful lighter-than-air, powered machine . . . my skill (ahem!) seems to derive from the great ace, B. Baron von Luckner.

The American part of my flying heritage comes directly from that great aviator Charles Lindbergh, known to all as the "Lone B. Eagle."

And maybe Amelia Beaglehart too!

What little ability I may possess at baseball probably came to me through genes inherited from the great George Herman "Beagle" Ruth.

It isn't generally known, I guess, that I am also very musical. Another happy accident of inheritance — this from the much revered Ludwig van Beagle.

The rain is really coming down now and I must close because the paper is getting wet but you should know that family legend has it that we are also connected to Supreme Court Justice Louis Dembitz Beagle, Senator Tom Beagleton and (sniff!) the entire ruling family of Europe, the celebrated House of Hapsbeagle.

Woodstock says ' ' ' '

YRS.

The Greyhound

The "as a" dog. If we didn't have this peachereeno, we couldn't say things like "swift as a," "keen-sighted as a," "sleek as a" or "graceful as a."

If you insist on discussing where everybody comes from you can tell your friends that your greyhound can be traced back to 3500 B.C. Pharaohs were nuts about them. That's how we know because a pharaoh could say to a guy, "Carve me my dog in stone, there." And the guy would do it. So all you have to do to show how far back it was is to take one of those carvings and give it the old Carbon 14 test. Right away it comes up 3500 B.C.

Pharaohs used them for chasing gazelles. Which is what they're *for*, for goodness' sake. They're not supposed to be down in Florida running after fake rabbits at racetracks. Humiliating.

It's funny, but Xenophon the Elder described the greyhound and mentioned that the celts called them "Veltragus." Means hare-catcher.

The French say that the more it changes, the more it's the same thing. A lot of French folks are Celts, especially the Bretons.

So you see.

Did you realize that the greyhound is the only dog that hunts by sight? They used to do it the other way like everybody else but it was bred out of them. Can you really breed out one of the five senses? Yes. You can do it in about a thousand years.

Now you'd better sit down. In the fifteenth century, in *The Boke of St. Albans*, Juliana Berners, Prioress of Sopewell Nunnery, wrote this:

> The Greyhound should be headed like a Snake,
> Footed like a Cat,
> Tailed like a Rat,
> Sided like a Teme,
> And chined like a Beme.

She talked funny.

Some people call whippets greyhounds. They are partly wrong.

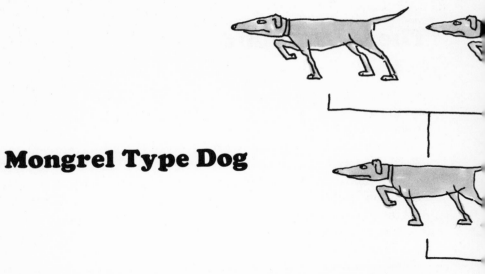

Mongrel Type Dog

This is your patchwork kind of friend. He is made of spare parts. Like many of us, his folks didn't think too much about Planned Parenthood. Like most of us, his blood lines are blurred.

And, like most of us, he is the most kind of dog there is.

Well, genealogy isn't everything. When you stop to think of it very few people can trace their ancestry back to Beowulf. And a lot of us are lucky if we can get past Calvin Coolidge.

When somebody says to somebody else, "Just what kind of dog is that?" and the somebody else replies, "Oh, he's half and half," that isn't the half of it. The reason for this is that each of the halves is probably nothing to write the American Kennel Club about.

A purebred dog may be too much of a good thing. You take your average, pedigreed, certified, vouched for and sworn to and testified animal and you'll find you've got a snob on your hands. Mister elegance won't lower himself to, say, chase a rabbit. Why should he? He's accustomed to three-minute eggs, moist pâté de foie gras — but not *too* moist — and things like brandy and after-dinner cigars. Rabbits, he thinks, are for the underadvantaged.

One of the first things we noticed about the average mongrel is that there isn't any. Still, they do have one thing in common. Even though they come in one million shapes and sizes and colors, they are all wonderful because each and every one of them fits a kid.

BOOTH

Puppy

Please stop saying that the puppy is cute. It's a complete waste of breath, it's redundant, it's tautological and nobody is listening anyway. They're just sitting around smiling at the puppy.

Did you ever see one that was un-cute?

Try these instead: frolicsome, larking, bouncy, inquisitive, floppy, amiable — no, nobody's listening anyway.

You read a lot about the Taj Mahal, the Grand Canyon, Paris in the spring . . . well, if you've never seen a baby dog who things he has five feet and can't find any of them, you ain't seen nothing. You may think you should go look at the tower of Pisa or the Russian steppes or Pittsburgh, but you'd have a better time just staying around the house with a small dog.

Try these: adorable, charming, volatile, inquisitive, frisky, trembly, eager, winsome — by George, you want somebody to listen to you you'll just have to get that pup out of the room.

There are a lot of dogs of whom practically nobody has ever heard of. A few of the kinds you never heard of are Transcaucasian Owtscharka, the, a kind of borzoi called a Tschelischtchev, the Perdigeiro of Portugal, the, the Schafpudel and the Xoloitcuintli. They exist, all right. And they have puppies. And I'll tell you something. All their puppies, without exception, are cute.

Napoleon's Favorite

The word "knee" comes from the Sanskrit "janu," meaning "elbow." Their word for knee actually means "hole in the ground." To this day many translators are accused, successfully, of not knowing their elbow from a hole in the ground.

Well, never mind the grammar. What is important is that Napoleon was a great leader of soldiers but he had either a bad stomach or some kind of pain that made him keep one hand inside his vest. Worse than that, he had cold knees. (French "genoux"; see above. Or, forget it.)

All right. Sometimes in a battle a general will get cold feet. Not Bonaparte (Napoleon). He got cold knees. All kinds of research says so. What they don't know is that the General (Napoleon) had cold knees — not before or during battle, but *all the time*.

BOOTH.

Lundi, Mardi, Mercredi, Janvier, Février, la quatorze Juillet . . . you name it. (C'est à vous.) Genoux froids.

Napoleon's docteur, a certain M. Frisson, had a bright idea . . . or maybe it wasn't but it worked. He got hold of a special breed of French-type dog that was noted for its body heat — a celebrated show dog called a Chien Chaud. M. Frisson trained the brave fella to lie down (s'accoucher), to roll over (se brouiller) and to play dead (jouer mort).

He also trained him to keep Napoleon's knees warm. In three short lessons! (Trois leçons courtes!)

"Well," you may say, "I never heard that!"

Tant pis.

The Coach Dog (TWO KINDS)

1. This is the common, spotted coach dog, or Dalmatian, which likes to run along beside or, preferably, under a coach. As there are now fewer coaches than almost ever, the coach dog has taken to hanging around firehouses. Or at least they did until firemen gave up having horses and turned to the internal combustion engine. So there are no more coach dogs of type (1).

2. This is a *real* coach dog that spends most of his time in coaching other dogs. Whenever a dog is unsure of just how to go about something, or just feels like "working out," he goes to a coach. Sometimes, especially among older dogs, they'll come back just to chew the fat. Very often when you see two dogs together and they appear to be doing nothing in particular, the chances are that they're a coach and one of his students, either a fairly new one or, quite likely, an old one come back to reminisce.

Take the familiar expression "Like a dog worrying a bone." Well, dogs, like other people, have relatively few instincts. They have to be taught how to make a bone worry. This is just one of a coach's many jobs.